Meet the Horses

Tennessee Walking Horses

by Rachel Grack

Ideas for Parents and Teachers

Bullfrog Books let children practice reading informational text at the earliest reading levels. Repetition, familiar words, and photo labels support early readers.

Before Reading

- Discuss the cover photo. What does it tell them?
- Look at the picture glossary together. Read and discuss the words.

During Reading

- "Walk" through the book with the reader. Discuss new or unfamiliar words. Sound them out together.
- Look at the photos together. Point out the photo labels.

After Reading

- Prompt the child to think more. Ask: Have you ever seen a Tennessee walking horse? What did it look like?

Bullfrog Books are published by Jump!
3500 American Blvd W, Suite 150
Bloomington, MN 55431
www.jumplibrary.com

Jump! is a division of FlutterBee Education Group.

Library of Congress Cataloging-in-Publication Data

Names: Koestler-Grack, Rachel A., 1973- author
Title: Tennessee walking horses / by Rachel Grack.
Description: Bloomington, MN: Jump!, Inc., [2026]
Series: Meet the horses | Includes index.
Audience: Ages 5–8
Identifiers: LCCN 2025016724 (print)
LCCN 2025016725 (ebook)
ISBN 9798896622444 (hardcover)
ISBN 9798896622451 (paperback)
ISBN 9798896622468 (ebook)
Subjects: LCSH: Tennessee walking horse—Juvenile literature
Classification: LCC SF293.T4 K64 2026 (print)
LCC SF293.T4 (ebook)
DDC 636.1/3—dc23/eng/20250818
LC record available at https://lccn.loc.gov/2025016724
LC ebook record available at https://lccn.loc.gov/2025016725

Editor: Katie Chanez
Designer: Molly Ballanger
Content Consultant: Becky Robb Hotzler; Wells Creek Wild Mustang Sanctuary; This Old Horse, Inc.

Photo Credits: Juniors Bildarchiv GmbH/Alamy, cover, 12–13, 14–15, 23bm; Horse Crazy/Shutterstock, 1; MWORTHI/iStock, 3; Shawn Hamilton/Shutterstock, 4; Eyal Bartov/Alamy, 5; Juniors Bildarchiv/juniors@wildlife Bildagentur GmbH/SuperStock, 8, 9, 19, 23tl, 23tm; Petra Eckerl/Adobe Stock, 10–11, 23bl; CRobertson/iStock, 16, 23br; Donald Page/Getty, 16–17; Larry Martin/Dreamstime, 18, 23tr, 24; Audrey Taylor/Alamy, 20–21; Shawn Hamilton CLiX/Adobe Stock, 22.

Printed in the United States of America at Corporate Graphics in North Mankato, Minnesota.

Table of Contents

Walking Horses

Horses walk.

They are Tennessee walking horses!

They come from Tennessee.

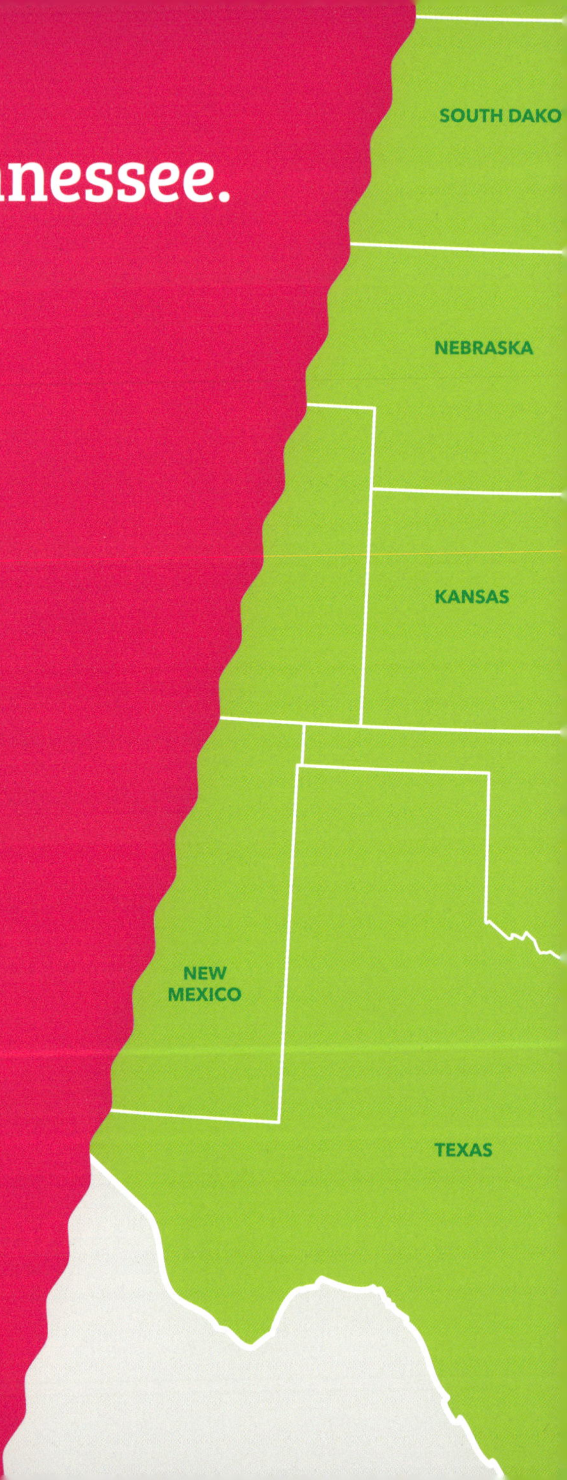

MINNESOTA
WISCONSIN
MICHIGAN
NEW YORK
PENNSYLVANIA
IOWA
OHIO
MARYLAND
INDIANA
ILLINOIS
WEST VIRGINIA
VIRGINIA
MISSOURI
KENTUCKY
NORTH CAROLINA
TENNESSEE
OKLAHOMA
ARKANSAS
SOUTH CAROLINA
GEORGIA
ALABAMA
MISSISSIPPI
LOUISIANA
FLORIDA
N
W
E
S

These horses can be many colors. Wolf's **coat** is **chestnut**.

Buster's coat is white.

It has spots.

These horses have their own **gait**.

It is a running walk.

They move smoothly.

Riders do not bounce.

Sky is in a show.

He **performs**.

He steps high.

Very good!

Bea goes to a football game.

Where?

The **University** of Tennessee!

I see **foals.**

They play!

Soda is ready to go!

Giddy up!

A Look at a Tennessee Walking Horse

What are the parts of a Tennessee walking horse? Take a look!

Picture Glossary

chestnut
A horse with a red-brown coat.

coat
The hair on a horse.

foals
Young horses.

gait
The way a horse walks or runs.

performs
Entertains an audience.

university
A place where people study for degrees beyond high school.

Index

To Learn More

Finding more information is as easy as 1, 2, 3.

1. Go to **www.factsurfer.com**
2. Enter "**Tennessee walking horses**" into the search box.
3. Choose your book to see a list of websites.